SWU-NAP- 011

UNIFORMS OF RUSSIAN ARMY DURING THE NAPOLEONIC WAR VOL.6

UNDER THE REIGN OF PAUL I
EMPEROR OF RUSSIA BETWEEN 1796 AND 1801
GUARDS 2

From the Viskovatov's greatest work:
"Historical description of the clothing and
arms of the Russian Army"

English translation by Mark Conrad

SOLDIER SHOP PUBLISHING

AUTHOR

Aleksandr Vasilevich Viskovatov born 22 April (4 May New Style) 1804, died 27 February (11 March) 1858 in St. Petersburg, Russian military historian. He graduated from the 1st Cadet Corps and served in the artillery, the hydrographic depot of the Naval Ministry, and then in the Department of Military Educational Institutions. He mainly studied historical artifacts and the histories of military units. Viskovatov's greatest work was the Historical Description of the Clothing and Arms of the Russian Army.

TRANSLATOR

Mark Conrad is an American historian with a great interest for all the Russian history.

Title: **UNIFORMS OF RUSSIAN ARMY DURING THE NAPOLEONIC WAR VOL. 6 - Guards 2 1796-1801**
By A.V. Viskovatov. English translation by Mark Conrad. First edition by Soldiershop.
Cover & Art Design: Luca S. Cristini. Plates re-colorations by Anna Cristini
ISBN code: 978-88-93270809

Published by Soldiershop publishing, via Padre Davide, 7 - 24050 Zanica (BG) ITALY. www.soldiershop.com

UNIFORMS
OF THE RUSSIAN
ARMY DURING THE
NAPOLEONIC WAR VOL.6

UNDER THE REIGN OF PAUL I EMPEROR OF
RUSSIA BETWEEN 1796 AND 1801

*

Guards 2 1796-1801

HISTORICAL DESCRIPTION OF THE CLOTHING AND ARMS
OF THE RUSSIAN ARMY - A.V. VISKOVATOV
(First English translation by Mark Conrad)

Soldiershop is glad to presents the complete collection of the great job made by A.V. Viskovatov dedicated to the uniforms and weapons belonging to the Russian army during the Napoleonic period, until 1825. The time we considered corresponds to the reigns of two Tzars: Paul I, who reigned since 1769 until his murder on the 23rd of March 1801, and his son Aleksandr Pavlovi☐ Romanov, that with the title of Alexander I, sat on the throne until the 1st December 1825.
Our reprint in based on the original 19th century volumes, to be precise the volumes from 7 to 9 are dedicated to the reign of Paul I; this first part is distributed on 7 volumes, having a numbering from 1 to 7. From number 10 to 18 of the original volumes, the second part is dedicated to the Russian troops under Alexander I. These still being worked on and they will be soon ready, distributed on twenty volumes approximately. Our new edition, the first ever published in English, both on paper and digital format, boasts a large number of color plates, many of them unpublished and coloured by our team of expert artists and scholars of uniformology. Each volume is based on 50/70 plates, always accompanied by the original translated text which describes the uniforms, the organization and the armament of the Russian army of the period.

A unique work in its genre, a must have in any respecting collection!
Aleksandr Vasilevich Viskovatov born 22 April (4 May New Style) 1804, died 27 February (11 March) 1858 in St. Petersburg, Russian military historian. He graduated from the 1st Cadet Corps and served in the artillery, the hydrographic depot of the Naval Ministry, and then in the Department of Military Educational Institutions.
He mainly studied historical artifacts and the histories of military units. Viskovatov's greatest work was the Historical Description of the Clothing and Arms of the Russian Army (Vols. 1-30, St. Petersburg, 1841-62; 2nd ed. Vols. 1-34, St. Petersburg - Novosibirsk - Leningrad, 1899-1948). This work is based on a great quantity of archival documents and contains four thousand colored illustrations.
Viskovatov was the author of Chronicles of the Russian Army (Books 1-20, St. Petersburg, 1834-42) and Chronicles of the Russian Imperial Army (Parts 1-7, St. Petersburg, 1852). He collected valuable material on the history of the Russian navy which went into A Short Overview of Russian Naval Campaigns and General Voyages to the End of the XVII Century (St. Petersburg, 1864; 2nd edition Moscow, 1946). Together with A.I. Mikhailovskii-Danilevskii he helped prepare and create the Military Gallery in the Winter Palace.
He wrote the historical military inscriptions for the walls of the Hall of St. George in the Great Palace of the Kremlin. (From the article in the Soviet Military Encyclopedia.)

CONTENTS

*

Preface pag. 5

*

Russian Army: Guards Infantry and Cavalry 2 pag. 7

*

Notes pag. 19

*

PLATES pag. 23

RUSSIAN ARMY,
Guards Artillery; Military Educational Institutions, Irregular and National Troops, Military Administration, Provincial Companies, Retired Personnel, and Orderlies
1796-1801

Contents

Changes in the uniforms and equipment of the Guards, Military Educational Establishments, Cossack and National forces, various separate commands, and military personnel not part of the Army, from 1796 to 1801:

XII. GUARDS ARTILLERY *(GVARDEISKAYA ARTILLERIYA)*

Throughout almost the entire reign of EMPEROR PAUL I, the uniforms and weapons of the Guards Artillery, horse as well as foot, and of the Pioneer, Pontoon, and Train detachments with it, were the same as in the Field Artillery, Pioneer Regiment, and Pontoon Depots. Only in **April 1800** was the Life-Guards Artillery Battalion given gold buttonhole loops on their cuff flaps: for lower ranks—of galloon; for officers—embroidered. The latter also received gold aiguilettes (*aksel'banty*) (Illus. 1189) [89].

XIII. MILITARY EDUCATIONAL ESTABLISHMENTS *(VOENNO-UCHEBNYYA ZAVEDENIYA)*

1 January 1797, *enrolled cadets of the Army* (later 1st) *Cadet Corps (stroevye kadety Sukhoputnago (v posledstvii 1-go) Kadetskago Korpusa)* were given dark-green cloth coats *(kaftany)* with red cloth collars, lapels, and slit cuffs, with red lining and brass buttons, of which six were on each side of the lapel and three under the right lapel and on the sleeves in the cuff slit (Illus. 1190). *Waistcoats* and *pants*were straw colored; white *parade gaiters (paradnyya shtiblety)*; black *everyday gaiters (vsednevnyya shtiblety)* and *neckcloths (galstuki)*. *Musketeers* wore tricorn *hats*: on parade—with narrow gold galloon, and for everyday use—without galloon, but at both times with three worsted tassels, green with a red interior (Illus. 1190). *Grenadiers* wore the same *caps* as army grenadiers except lower in height and with a plate and three grenades of gilt brass *(iz mednoi, vyzolochennoi latuni)*. The back of the cap was straw-colored, the band red, and the trim gold galloon with black silk, as in the Guards (Illus. 1190). *Accouterments* and *weapons* were of the patterns in use throughout the infantry [90].

Non-commissioned officers, as opposed to cadets, were prescribed the same distinctions as non-commissioned officers had relative to privates in the army. Halberd shafts were coffee-colored[91]. *Drummers* in *Musketeer* and *Grenadier companies; fifers* in *Grenadier companies; Corps drummers* and *musicians*: these had sewn-on stripes made of yellow worsted tape with red edges and likewise red checks in the center [92].

Officers had a uniform patterned after those for cadets, but with nine buttons on each side of the lapels, and on their hats—wide crenellated galloon, a cockade, and a buttonhole loop (Illus. 1191). For them alone in the whole Russian Army were kept *gorgets* of the pattern confirmed at the opening of the Corps in 1732, except now without the differences for ranks that were formerly in use, as for all grades they were silver with a gold edge, and they were worn not on a sky-blue tape, but on one that was black with orange edges. Shafts for officer spontoons were coffee-colored [93].

Cadets of the Boys' Section (Maloletnoe Otdelenie) were given double-breasted *jackets (kamzol'chiki)* with covered buttons, long *pants (shtany)* worn buttoned to the jacket; individually sized round-toed *shoes (bashmaki)* with brass buckles, and three-cornered *hats* without any decoration except a cord to bind them up (Illus. 1192). These *hats* were authorized only for holidays and when outside the Corps; during the rest of the time they were replaced by cloth *forage caps* the same color as the jacket and pants, with a red band and a tassel of dark green mixed with white (Illus. 1192). For *winter* the jackets and pants were made of cloth or baize *(iz sukna ili iz baiki)*. These did not stay the same color, and not everyone wore identical colors at the same time: dark and light green, not infrequently sky blue, but mostly black, while in summer—of white Flemish linen. (Illus. 1192 and 1193). During freezing weather and when on leave from the Corps—in winter and summer—cadets wore over the jacket baize *frock coats (sertuki)* of the above mentioned colors, with a low standing collar and one row of covered buttons (Illus. 1192). During winter, when wearing the *kamzol'chik* as well as the *kurtka* jacket, each cadet was issued a pair of suede *gloves* with wool inserts, sewn to the ends of a particolored—or of any color whatsoever—woven tape which passed over the nape of the neck and under the armpits to bed thrown over the back with one end over the other (Illus. 1193). Cadets in the enrolled line companies powdered their hair and wore curls and queues, while in the Boys' Section powder was not used and hair was worn without curls and queues [94].

Since **1 January 1798**, *cadets* and *officers* of the *Artillery and Engineer* (later the 2nd) *Cadet Corps* received uniform clothing similar to that which the Field Artillery had, except with red cuffs instead of dark green, and with the addition of red cloth lapels and—for parades—white linen gaiters. A final difference was that officers' waistcoats had no galloon (Illus. 1194) [95].

1798 December 23 – Uniforms were confirmed for the newly established *IMPERIAL Military Orphans' Home* (*IMPERATORSKII Voenno-Sirotskii Dom*):

a) *for cadets* – dark-green *caftan coat*, *waistcoat*, and *pants*, with brass buttons. The coat had a red collar, round cuffs, and lining; white *parade pants* and *gaiters and summer waistcoat*; black *neck cloth* and *everyday gaiters*; round-toed *shoes*; *hat* with narrow gold galloon and three tassels of green and—in the center—white worsted (Illus. 1195) [96].

b) *for pupils who were soldiers' children (vospitanniki iz soldatskikh detei)* – the same everyday wear as for cadets, but the neckcloth was *red* with white trim, and the *hat* had no decoration (Illus. 1196) [97].

c) *for students in the Military Orphans' Sections (uchenikii Voenno-Sirotskikh Otdelenii)* – dark-green frock coat (*sertuk*) with a red standing collar, and with brass buttons down both sides of the chest; black *neckcloth*; round-toed *shoes*; dark-green *forage cap* (Illus. 1197). No underwear was issued by the government, but it was made up as the command administration saw fit [98].

Officers of the Military Orphans' Sections had uniforms of the same colors as for cadets and *hats* with narrow galloon (Illus. 1198) [99].

1799 October 31 – The directive that ordered officers' sashes, sword knots, and hat tassels have raspberry added to the black and orange silk was extended to cadet officers [100].

From **1 January 1800** – The *1st Cadet Corps*, and from **13 April** also the *2nd Cadet Corps*, were ordered to have: *coats*, as before, dark green with lapels, cuffs, and lining, with a dark-green standing collar and white buttons; *waistcoat* and *pants*, as previously, straw-colored; black *neckcloths*; *hats* with binding and a buttonhole loop of narrow silver galloon, and with an officer's cockade (Illus. 1199). On their lapels, cuffs, sleeve flaps, and waistline, *officers* had buttonhole loops of fine silver cord with small tassels, and on the hat—wide silver galloon with crennelations, a buttonhole loop, and a cockade (Illus. 1199) [101]. The *Shklov Cadet Corps* also received this exact same uniform [102].

XIV. IRREGULAR TROOPS (IRREGULYARNYYA VOISKA)

In regard to irregular forces, under EMPEROR PAUL I there were changes in the uniform of only the *Chuguev* and *Teptyar* regiments and *Leib-Ural Sotnya*.

On **9 January 1798**, the *1st* and *2nd Chuguev Regiments* were given clothing of leib-cossack pattern, except with a low standing collar and diagonal hussar cuffs on the *caftan coats* as well as the *half-caftans (polukaftany)*. The latter were red with cords, galloon, and buttons sewn on exactly as on hussar dolmans. *Shirovary* pants, *headdress bags*, and *saddlecloths* were also red. *Boots* were black for lower ranks, yellow for officers. *Accouterments* and *weapons* were the same as for Leib-Cossacks

(Illus. 1200). Outer *kaftan* coats were black with red lining and trimmed—for lower ranks—with tape (*tes'ma*) along the edges of the collar and cuffs, and for officers—additionally down the coat's front opening, with galloon (*galun*) (Illus. 1200a). *In the 1st Chuguev Regiment* all sewn-on trim and buttons were yellow (gold for officers). *In the 2nd Chuguev Regiment*—white (silver for officers) (Illus. 1200 and 1200a). In regard to weapons, Chuguev cossacks were distinguished from Leib-Cossacks only in having a *carbine* instead of a pistol [103].

From **11 October 1798**, the *1st* and *2nd Teptyar Regiments* were uniformed and armed similar to the Chuguev regiments, but without buttons, cord trim, and other sewn-on trim, and they had another style of headdress. They had *kaftan* coats and *polukaftan* undress coats of dark-blue cloth, *shirovary* pants of black cloth, and *girdles* (*kushaki*) of straw-colored cloth with red trim along the edges (Illus. 1201). *Headdresses* (*shapki*) were of dark-blue cloth with a black band, but it is unknown what these actually looked like [104].

The *Leib-Ural Sotnia*, along with the same weapons and same patterns of clothing as for Leib-Cossacks, had, since **1798**, raspberry *kaftan* coats with thin galloon trim—white for lower ranks and silver for officers. *Undress coats* (*polukaftan'ya*) and *shirovary* pants were also raspberry but without any trim or decoration. *Headdresses*, also raspberry, were square at the bottom and pointed at the top, with a wide band of black astrakhan (*smushka*) (Illus. 1202). *Shabracks* (*chepraki*) were raspberry, trimmed around with white tape (silver galloon for officers) [105].

XV. NATIONAL TROOPS (*NATSIONAL'NAYA VOISKA*)

On **9 June 1797**, the *Lithuanian Tatar Horse Regiment* (*Litovskii Tatarskii Konnyi polk*) was prescribed the following clothing, arms, and horse furniture:

Rankers (*sherengovye*) or privates (*ryadovye*) – red cloth *jacket* (*dulam*) with very dark-blue (*temno-sinii*) cloth collar and cuffs; *shirovary pants* likewise of very dark-blue cloth; *boots* with blunt toes and driven-in spurs; *girdle* of green (later yellow) stamin; black *neckcloth*; deerskin *gloves*, yellowish in color, with gauntlet cuffs; *headdress* of black astrakhan iwht a red cloth top, red worsted cords and tassels, and a tall white plume of fine feathers; hussar *saber* with iron hilt and scabbard; *sword knot, sword belt, cartridge pouch*, and *cartridge-pouch belt* of red Russianleather, stitched along the edges with white thread; brass *sword-belt buckles* and *rings*, and likewise the rings, buckles, slide, and endpiece of the cartridge pouch; yellow deerskin *cross belt* with brass buckle, slide, and endpiece, and an iron hook to carry the pistol; *pistol* with brass fittings; hussar *saddle*; red cloth *shabrack* with toothed trim of very dark-blue cloth, and white cord along the edges of the teeth; very dark-blue cloth *valise* (Illus. 1203) [106].

Comrades (*tovarishchi*)—red cloth *jacket* with collar and cuffs of very-dark blue cloth, trimmed with thin white cord and, on the chest, with white buttonhole loops and small tassels. Very dark-blue *shirovary* pants with white cord on the side seams and along the lower edge; *girdle, neckcloth, gloves*, and *headdress* the same as for rankers but with white and white worsted cords and tassels on the last item instead of all red. Hussar-pattern *saber* with green scabbard and iron hilt and mountings; *sword knot, sword belt, cartridge pouch, cartridge-pouch belt*, two *pistols, saddle, shabrack*, and *valise*—all the same as for rankers. *Lance* with red shaft and a pennon (*khoronchevka* or *znachok*) that was dark blue above and red below (Illus. 1204) [107].

Non-commissioned officers (namestniki, literally "deputies"))—red cloth jacket with collar and cuffs of very dark-blue cloth, with white buttonhole loops and small tassels on the chest and silver galloon along the edges of the collar and cuffs. *Shirovary* pants, *boots, girdle, neckcloth, gloves,* and *headdress* the same as for comrades, with the only differences being that the last item had all-white cords and tassles, while the plume was white with a black top. Reed *canes* (Illus. 1204). *Accouterments* and *weapons* the same as for comrades except that lances were not prescribed for deputies [108].

Officers—red cloth *jacket* with collar and cuffs of very dark-blue cloth, trimmed with thin silver cord, and with silver buttonhole loops and small tassels on the chest; very dark-blue *shirovary* pants trimmed along the side seams and at the bottom with thin silver cord; silver *girdle* with a mix of black and orange silk, and with two tassels fastened to the left side; *boots, neckcloth, gloves,* and *headdress* the same as for the preceding ranks, but the last item having silver cords and tassels and a white feather plume with black feathers toward the bottom; *saber* of the pattern prescribed for lower ranks; *sword knot* of black leather with silver stitching and tassel; *sword belt* and *cartridge pouch* of red morocco, with silver stitching; *cartridge-pouch belt* likewise of red morocco with silver galloon sewn on over almost its entire width; *sword-belt buckles* and *rings*, as well as *buckles, slide, endpiece,* and *rings* for the cartridge pouch—all gilt; reed *cane*; *pistols* with brass mountings; *shabrack* the same as for lower ranks but with thin silver cord along the tooth pattern (Illus. 1205) [109].

For winter, all of the above mentioned ranks were prescribed dark-blue cloth *undress coats (polukaftan'ya)* with the same cuffs and collar as on the jacket, but in red. For *rankers* these coats were without any kind of trim (Illus. 1206); for *comrades*—with white trim along the edges of the collar, cuffs, front opening, skirts, and pocket flaps, with likewise white buttonhole loops and small tassels, and turned-back skirts, as on the undress Hungarian coats for hussar officers (Illus. 1206); for *deputies*—similar to the preceding but with silver galloon on the collar and cuffs (Illus. 1206); for *officers*—with thin silver cord around the collar, cuffs, front opening, skirts, and pocket flaps, and likewise silver buttonhole loops and small tassels, and turned-back skirts (Illus. 1206) [110].

Combatant ranks in the *Polish Horse Regiment (Pol'skii konnyi polk)* had the following uniform, accouterments, and horse furniture:

Rankers (sherengovye)—red cloth *undress coat (polukaftan'e)*or jacket *(kurtka)* (of the style introduced in the Russian army by Prince Potemkin) with a standing collar, slit cuffs, and turned-back skirts of very dark-blue cloth, trimmed with thing white cord, and with white buttons. *Shirovary* pants of very dark-blue cloth, with thin white cord on the sides and below; *boots, neckcloth,* and *gloves* the same as for the preceding regiment. *Headdress (shapka)* with a quilted crown of red cloth, a dark-blue band slit on the left side, white cord around this band, and with a likewise white feathe plume. *Saber* of hussar style, with iron hilt and scabbard; *sword knot, sword belt, cartridge pouch,* and *crossbelt* (used instead of a cartridge-pouch belt)—all yellow deersking. *Belt plate* in the front of the sword belt (with a two-headed eagle depicted in relief), all *rings, buckles, slide,* and *endpiece*—tinned brass *(mednye, vyluzhennye)*. *Pistol* with brass mountings. Red *shabrack* with crenellation, two-headed eagles, and IMPERIAL monograms of black cloth, these being trimmed all around with thin white cord. *Saddle* and other appurtenences—the same as described above for the Lithuanian Tatar Regiment (Illus. 1207)[111].

Comrades (tovarishchi)—undress coat, pants, boots, neckcloth, gloves, headdress, saber, sword knot, sword belt, cartridge pouch, cartridge-pouch belt, and all *horse furniture*—completely identical to that for rankers, from whom they were distinguished only in armament, since instead of a single pistol on a crossbelt hook they had two in holsters *(ol'stredi)* under the shabrack, and were additonally armed with a *lance (pika)* with a shaft painted with wide black and flesh-colored, or blanched, stripes and narrow white stripes *(okrashennye chernymi i blanzhevymi, shirokimi, i belymi, uzkimi polosami)*. It also had a *khoronchevka* pennon of the same three colors with an cross swen on in the center. The upper half of the pennon and the lower half of the cross were black; the lower half of the pennon and upper half of the cross—flesh-colored; edging around the pennon and cross—white (Illus. 1208)[112].

Deputies had the same as comrades except with the addition of silver galloon on the collar and cuffs and a second row of cord on the headdress band, and not having a lance, instead of which they were authorized a *cane* (Illus. 1209)[113].

Officers had uniforms of the same colors and pattern as prescribed for lower ranks, but having on the collar wide silver galloon with dark-blue silk interwoven down the middle, and silver buttonhole loops. The same galloon was on the cuffs and headdress, with the latter having likewise silver cords and galloon. Thin silver cord was also on the pants and jacket's skirts. The *saber* was the same as for lower ranks. The *sword knot* was of black leather, with silver. *Sword belt, cartridge pouch,* and *cartridge-pouch belt*—deerskin, with the same galloon as on the collar, with the last item also having two silver lines and chains *(protravniki i tsepochki)*. Gilt *sword-belt* and *cartridge-pouch buckles, slides, endpieces,* and *rings,* as well as the eagle on the sword-belt plate. *Girdle (kushak)* of silver and dark-blue silk, with two silver tassels in which was mixed black and orange silk. *Pistols* and *all horse furniture*—the same as for lower ranks, exceptthat shabracks had thin silver cord and likewise silver fringe around the monograms and on the edges (Illus. 1209). As all officers of that time, they were prescribed to have canes [114].

From **13 April 1797**, the *Balaklava Greek Infantry Battalion (Balaklavskii Grecheskii Pekhotnyi batalion)* was left with the same uniform clothing and weaponry as the second battalion of the Greek Infantry Regiment had under EMPRESS CATHERINE II, with only the change of red waistcoats to dark green, of green waistcoat collar and cuffs to red, of all-green spencers or jackets *(spenzery* or *kurtki)* to dark-green with red collar and lining, and of gold buttons on officers' waistcoats to silver. For *non-commissioned officers* the lower edge of the collar, both sides of the jacket opening, and both sides of the waistcoat opening, were trimmed with narrow gold galloon, somewhat wider for *officers* (Illus. 1210 and 1211) [115].

The regiments of **Prince de Condé's corps** which entered Russian service on **27 November 1797** were uniformed and armed exactly as regular Russian infantry and cavalry regiments. The colors prescribed for them were as follows:

a) *Prince de Condé's French Noble Regiment* – black velvet collar, lapels, and cuffs; gold buttonhole loops (7 on each lapel, 2 on each cuff flap, 3 on each pocket flap, 2 at the waist), with wire thread *(s bit'yu)* without any small tassels; straw-colored waistcoat and pants; black everyday gaiters, white for parade; hats with narrow gold lace; yellow buttons, gilded; coffee-colored shafts for halberds and spontoons (Illus. 1212) [116].

b) *Duke de Bourbon's French Grenadier Regiment* – black cloth collar, lapels, and cuffs; yellow buttonhole loops on cuff flaps (gold for officers, with small tassels and raspberry silk); white waistcoat and pants; yellow buttons; black gaiters; for lower ranks – straw-colored backs to grenadier caps, raspberry bands, trimmed yellow with black; for officers – hats with narrow gold galloon; coffee-colored shafts for halberds and spontoons (Illus. 1213) [117].

Duke de Hohenlohe's German Regiment – the same and the preceding regiment, but with white buttonhole loops, buttons, and galloon (Illus. 1214) [117].

Duke de Berry's Noble Dragoon Regiment – black cloth collar, lapels, and cuffs; gold buttonhole loops, with wire thread, without small tassels; yellow buttons (Illus. 1215) [119].

Duke d'Enghien's Dragoon Regiment – black cloth collar and cuffs; white buttons (Illus. 1216) [120].

Artillery officer at horse 1800

XVI. DETACHMENTS AT VARIOUS OFFICIAL PLACES AND GOVERNMENT BUILDINGS, AND OTHER SEPARATE UNITS UNDER THE MILITARY ADMINISTRATION (*V komandakh pri raznykh prisutstvennykh mestakh i kazennykh domakh i v drugikh otdel'nykh chastyakh voennago vedomstva*)

1796 December 13 and **1797 February 2** – *feldjägers (fel'd"-yegeri, or official couriers)* were given the exact same uniforms as officers in Dragoon regiments except for changing the ligh-green color of the *kaftan* coat to green, and the straw-colored lining to red. Their collar and cuffs were red cloth; gold aiguillette and buttons; straw-colored waistcoat which soon became green; cavalry sword with silver sword knot. Simple feldjägers as well as *officers* were authorized canes, and the latter were distinguished from the former only by having hats without plumes, with wide, toothed gold galloon (Illus. 1217) [121].

1797 February 16 – The *Senate Battalion* was given the exact same uniform and armament as already described above when (in 1800) they joined the list of Army Musketeer regiments [122].

1796 December 13 – The *Medical Orderlies Detachment at the Army Hospital (Sluzhitel'skaya komanda pri Sukhoputnom gospitale)*; **1797 November 2**– personnel of the *Invalid Detachment with the Senate's Land Survey Department (Invalidnaya komanda pri Mezhevom Senata Departamente)*; **1798 January 5** – *Commissariat and Provisions personnel (Kommissariatskie i Proviantskie sluzhiteli)*; **1798 April 21** – *Invalid detachments at the Olonets, Kronstadt, and Lugansk foundaries (Invalidnyya komandy pri Olonetskom, Kronshtadtskom i Luganskom liteinykh zavodakh*; **1799 April 16** – *Invalid detachments at the Postal Department and St.-Petersburg, Moscow, Little-Russian, Tambov, and Kazan post offices (Invalidnyya komandy pri Pochtovom Departamente i pri Pochamatakh: S.-Peterburgskom, Moskovskom, Mallorossiiskom, Tambovskom i Kazanskom*; and **1799 November 12** – *Invalid detachment at the St.-Petersburg city granaries (Invalidnaya komanda pri S.-Peterburgskikh gorodovykh ambarakh)*—the clothing, accouterments, and weapons for these were prescribed to be the same as for garrison invalids [123].

Mines battalions (gornozavodskie bataliony) kept the uniforms they received during the reign of EMPRESS CATHERINE II [124].

XVII. STATE PROVINCIAL COMPANIES AND DETACHMENTS (*SHTATNYYA GUBERNSKIYA ROTY I KOMANDY*)

1796 December 31; 1797 February 6, 19, and 26; 4 March – *State Provincial companies and detachments*, in regard to their uniforms and arms, were left as they were during the preceding reign [125].

1798 October 9 – A HIGHEST Order decreed that *kaftan* coats in all these companies and detachments be the same color—dark green—with collars, waistcoats, and nether garments in the colors prescribed for each province [126].

XVIII. PERSONNEL UNDER THE MILITARY ADMINISTRATION BUT NOT PART OF THE ARMY ITSELF (*Litsa voennago vedomstva, sobstvenno v sostav Armii ne vkhodivshikh*)

1796 November 16 and December 18 – *Personnel in the Military Collegium and Commissariat and Provisions Departments* were ordered to wear the uniform of the regiment from which they left to enter the administration [127].

1796 December 16 – For personnel not part of a particular regiment, but *assigned to the Army at large (sostoyavshie po Armii)*, a *standard Army uniform (obshchii armeiskii mundir)* was established. *For Infantry* – dark-green *kaftan* coat, without lapels, with red collar, slit cuffs, and lining (Illus. 1218). *For Cavalry* – white *caftan* coat, without lapels, with red collar, slit cuffs, and lining (Illus. 1219). In the *Infantry* – white neckcloth; hat with narrow gold galloon; infantry officer's sword (*shpaga*). In the *Cavalry* – black neckcloth; hat without galloon, with a buttonhole loop, cockade, and white plume black and orange at the base; and a cavalry officer's sword. In the *Infantry* and *Cavalry* – gold buttons and aiguillettes white waistcoats, deerskin breeches, boots with spurs, gloves with gauntlet cuffs; sashes, sword knots, and canes the same so for officers throughout the army [128].

1797 January 23 – The above-mentioned orders of 1769 November 16 and December 18 were applied only to those personnel of the *Military Collegium and Commissarriat and Provisions Departments* who would join those establishments in the future, while personnel already in these places were ordered to wear dark-green *coats* with cuffs and cuff flaps of that same color, without lapels, with a red cloth collar, green lining, and yellow buttons; white *waistcoat* and *breeches*; boots with spurs (Illus. 1220) [129].

1798 March 13 – All personnel and officials belonging to the *General-Auditoriat*, except for the General-Auditors, were given uniforms the same as those prescribed for regimental Auditors [130].

1798 December – *Officers of HIS IMPERIAL MAJESTY'S Suite for Quartermaster Affairs*, who were assigned *to the Infantry*, were ordered to wear a coat like that for field-grade officers of the Life-Guards Preobrazhenskii Regiment except without buttonhole loops, i.e. the standard army infantry uniform, while those assigned *to the Cavalry* had the standard army cavalry uniform [131].

1800 February 25 – *General officers of the Military Collegium (Generalitet Voennoi Kollegii)*, as well as of the *Commissariat and Provisions Departments (Kommissariatskii i Proviantskii Departamenty)*, were ordered to wear the *standard army uniform for infantry (obshchii armeiskii mundir po infanterii)*. The *General-Auditor* was prescribed the *standard army uniform for cavalry* while others *not holding military ranks (ne imevshie voennykh chinov)* had military-pattern uniforms newly established for them: dark-green with slit cuffs in that same color, with brass buttons and without a collar. *Waistcoats* and *breeches* with this coat were prescribed to be white. *Hats* were without galloon and tassels, and *swords (shpagi)* had no sword knots (Illus. 1221) [132].

1800 April 19 – All *officials on the authorized Commissariat and Provisions establishments* were prescribed to wear the uniforms of those administrations from which they came: *military officials—* military (*voennye*) uniforms, and *civilian officials—*civilian (*statskie*) uniforms [133].
General-Adjutants in the *Infantry* wore the *standard army uniform for infantry* with a gold aiguilette and similarly gold embroidery on the collar, cuff flaps, pocket flaps, waist, and also down the front opening (Illus. 1222) [134].

Infantry Aides-de-Camp (Fligel'-Ad"yutanty po Infanterii) wore a coat similar to the above, but with silver buttons, aiguilette, and embroidery (Illus. 1222) [135].

General-Adjutants in the *Cavalry* had the *standard army uniform for cavalry*, with a gold aiguilette and similarly gold embroidery on the collar, cuffs, pocket flaps, waist, and down the front opening (Illus. 1223) [136].

Cavalry Aides-de-Camp had the same uniform as General-Adjutants but with silver buttons, aiguilettes, and embroidery (Illus. 1223) [137].

XIX. RETIRED PERSONNEL *(OTSTAVNYE)*

1796 December 7 – Guards and all other *officers released from service since December 4th* of this year were ordered—except for those who received special permission by HIGHEST Authority—to not wear military uniforms, but rather use provincial civl uniforms (*mundiry gubernskie*) according to where they have estates [138].

1796 December 13 – All *generals and officers who retired before December 4th* of this year were permitted to wear the uniforms in which they served [139].

XX. ORDERLIES *(DEN'SHCHIKI)*

1797 August – *Orderlies (den'shchiki)* and *company and field-grade officers' own servants (sobstvennye lyudi)* were ordered to have dark-green clothing with collar and cuffs in the regimental facing color. The cut of the clothing was left up to the Honorary Colonel (*Shef*), but with the proviso that it not vary within an individual regiment [140].

(**1801 January 24** – Major General Cozens is reprimanded for having **orderlies** in his regiment wearing jackets (*kurtki*). It is confirmed for the whole Army that such a violation is not to be permitted (HIGHEST Order of 24 January 1801). - M.C.)

Russian Don Cossack during the raid of 9 August 1799 at Augsburg

NOTES

(89) The drawings cited above in Note 81; HIGHEST Confirmed table of uniforms, accouterments, and weapons for the Life-Guards Artillery Battalion; *Chronicle of the Russian Army*, compiled by Prince Dolgorukov, No 208, and statements by contemporaries.

(90) The drawings cited above in Note 81; *Chronicle of the Russian Army*, compiled by Prince Dolgorukov, No 7; HIGHEST Confirmed table of uniforms, accouterments, and weapons for the Army Cadet Corps, 10 March 1799, and statements by contemporaries.

(91) Ditto.

(92) Ditto.

(93) Ditto.

(94) Ditto.

(95) The drawings cited in Note 81; *Chronicle of the Russian Army*, compiled by Prince Dolgorukov, No 224, and statements by contemporaries.

(96) HIGHEST confirmed table of uniforms, accouterments, and weapons for the IMPERIAL Military Orphans' Home and its Sections, 23 December 1798, and statements by contemporaries.

(97) Ditto.

(98) Ditto.

(99) Ditto.

(100) PSZ Vol. XLIV, Part II, Sect. Four, under information on uniforms, page 3, No 19,178, and statements by contemporaries.

(101) Statements from persons who served in the 1st and 2nd Cadet Corps during the reign of EMPERORPAULI; drawings of uniforms of the 2nd Cadet Corps executed in the HIS IMPERIAL HIGHNESS the Inspector-General for Engineering's Own Drafting Establishment; drawings of uniforms executed in March 1800 by Maj.-Gen. Prince Dolgorukov and located in HIS IMPERIAL MAJESTY's Own Library catalogued under No 327, and PSZ, Vol. XLIV, Part II, Sect. IV, pgs. 2 and 4, No 19,379.

(102) The same books from PSZ and on the same pages, No 19,382.

(103) *Chronicle of the Russian Army*, compiled by Prince Dolgorukov, Nos 204 and 205, and drawings of uniforms located in HIS IMPERIAL MAJESTY's Own Library, catalogued under No 159.

(104) PSZ, Vol. XLIII, Pt. I, Sect. One, No 18,701, pg. 50.

(105) *Chronicle of the Russian Army*, compiled by Prince Dolgorukov, No 202; the uniform drawings cited above in Note 101, and drawings of the same uniforms located in HIS IMPERIAL MAJESTY's Own Library, catalogued under No 246.

(106) PSZ, Vol. XLIII, Pt. I, Sect. One, No 17,993, pg. 23; *Chronicle of the Russian Army*, compiled by Prince Dolgorukov, No 206, and drawings of uniforms of the Lithuanian-Tatar Regiment located in HIS IMPERIAL MAJESTY's Own Library in portfolio No 168.

(107) Ditto.

(108) Ditto.

(109) Ditto.

(110) Ditto.

(111) *Chronicle of the Russian Army*, compiled by Prince Dolgorukov, No 207, and drawings of uniforms of the Polish Horse Regiment located in HIS IMPERIAL MAJESTY's Own Library in portfolio No 168.

(112) Ditto.

(113) Ditto.

(114) Ditto.

(115) PSZ Vol. XLIII, pt. I, first section, No 17,915, pg. 20, and description, with drawings, of the uniform of the Balaklava Greek Battalion, received from the battalion Commander in August 1840.

(116) *Chronicle of the Russian Army*, compiled by Prince Dolgorukov, No 156, and this same number in the drawings located in HIS IMPERIAL MAJESTY's Own Library, catalogued under No 177.

(117) Ditto, No 157.

(118) Ditto, No 158.

(119) Ditto, No 194.

(120) Ditto, No 195.

(121) PSZ, Vol. XLIII, pt. I, first section, No 17,781, pg. 12, and drawings of uniforms located in HIS IMPE-RIAL MAJESTY's Own Library, catalogued under Nos 159 and 327.

(122) HIGHESTConfirmed table of uniforms, accouterments, and weapons for the Senate Battalion, *Chronicle of the Russian Army*, compiled by Prince Dolgorukov, No 159, and this same number in the drawings in HIS IMPERIAL MAJESTY's Own Library, catalogued under No 177.

(123) PSZ, Vol. XLIII, pt. I, first section, pg. 7; Vol. XLIV, pt. II, fourth section, No 17,987, pg. 301; Vol. XLIII, pt. I, first section, No 18,232, pg. 26, and No 18,308, pg. 28; Vol. XLIV, pt. II, fourth section, No 18,491, pg. 317; No 18,938, pg. 327 et seq., and No 19,189, pg. 351.

(124) Drawings located in HIS IMPERIAL MAJESTY's Own Library, catalogued under No 159.

(125) HIGHESTConfirmed organization tables for provinces: 31 December 1796; 6, 19, and 26 February, and 4 March, 1797.

(126) PSZ, Vol. XLIV, pt. II, fourth section, pgs. 2 and 5; No 18,699.

(127) Ibid., pgs. 1 and 4, Nos. 17,557 and 17,662.

(128) Ibid, pgs. 1 and 3, No 17,653; drawings located in HIS MAJESTY THE SOVEREIGN EMPEROR's Own Library, catalogued under No 327, and statements from contemporaries.

(129) Ibid., pgs. 2 and 4, No 17,555, and statements from contemporaries.

(130) Ibid, pgs. 2 and 4, No 18,342.

(131) Ibid., pgs. 2 and 4, No 18,810, and statements from contemporaries.

(132) Drawings of Russian military uniforms in 1800, compiled by Maj.-Gen. Prince Dolgorukov and located in HIS MAJESTY THE SOVEREIGN EMPEROR's Own Library, catalogued under No 327, and statements from contemporaries.

(133) PSZ, Vol. XLIV, pt. II, fourth section, pgs. 2 and 4; No 19,391.

(134) The drawings cited in Note 132, and statements from contemporaries.

(135) Ditto.

(136) Ditto.

(137) Ditto.

(138) PSZ, Vol. XLIV, pt. II, fourth section, pgs. 1 and 4; No 17,619.

(139) Ibid., pgs. 1 and 4, No 17,642.

(140) Ibid., pgs. 2 and 5, No 18,122.

Ruſſiſch Kaiſerl. Tartaren und Doniſche Coſacken

РИСУНКИ
Одежды и Вооруженія
РОССІЙСКИХЪ
ВОЙСКЪ.

PLATES LIST OF ILLUSTRATIONS

1206. Ranker and Comrade. Lithuanian-Tatar Horse Regiment, 1797-1801. (In winter uniform.)

1206a. Non-Commissioned Officer and Officer. Lithuanian-Tatar Horse Regiment, 1797-1801. (In winter uniform.)

1208. Comrade. Polish Horse Regiment, 1797-1801.

1209. Officer and Non-Commissioned Officer. Polish Horse Regiment, 1797-1801.

1210. Non-Commissioned Officer and Private. Balaklava Greek Infantry Battalion, 1797-1830.

1211. Officer. Balaklava Greek Infantry Battalion, 1797-1801.

1212. Musketeer and Company-Grade Officer. Prince de Condé's French Noble Regiment, 1797-1800.

1213. Company-Grade Officer and Non-Commissioned Officer. Duke de Bourbon's French Grenadier Regiment, 1797-1800.

1214. Field-Grade Officer. Duke de Hohenlohe's German Regiment, 1797-1800.

1215. Officer and Private. Duke de Berry's Noble Dragoon Regiment, 1797-1800.

1216. Non-Commissioned Officer and Officer. Duke d'Enghien's Dragoon Regiment, 1797-1800.

1217. Feldjäger and Feldjäger Officer. 1797-1801.

1218. Officer in standard Army uniform for Infantry, 1796-1801.

1219. Officer in standard Army uniform for Cavalry, 1796-1801.

1220. Officer. Military Collegium and Commissariat and Provisions Departments, 1797-1801.

1221. Official. Military Collegium and Commissariat and Provisions Departments, 1800-1801.

1222. General-Adjutant and Aide-de-Camp. Infantry, 1796-1801.

1223. Aide-de-Camp and General-Adjutant. Cavalry, 1796-1801.

Leib-Hussar. 1796-1798. (In parade uniform.)

Non-Commissioned Officers and Trumpeter. Leib-Hussar Regiment, 1796-1798.

Leib-Hussar Officer. 1796-1798. (In parade uniform.)

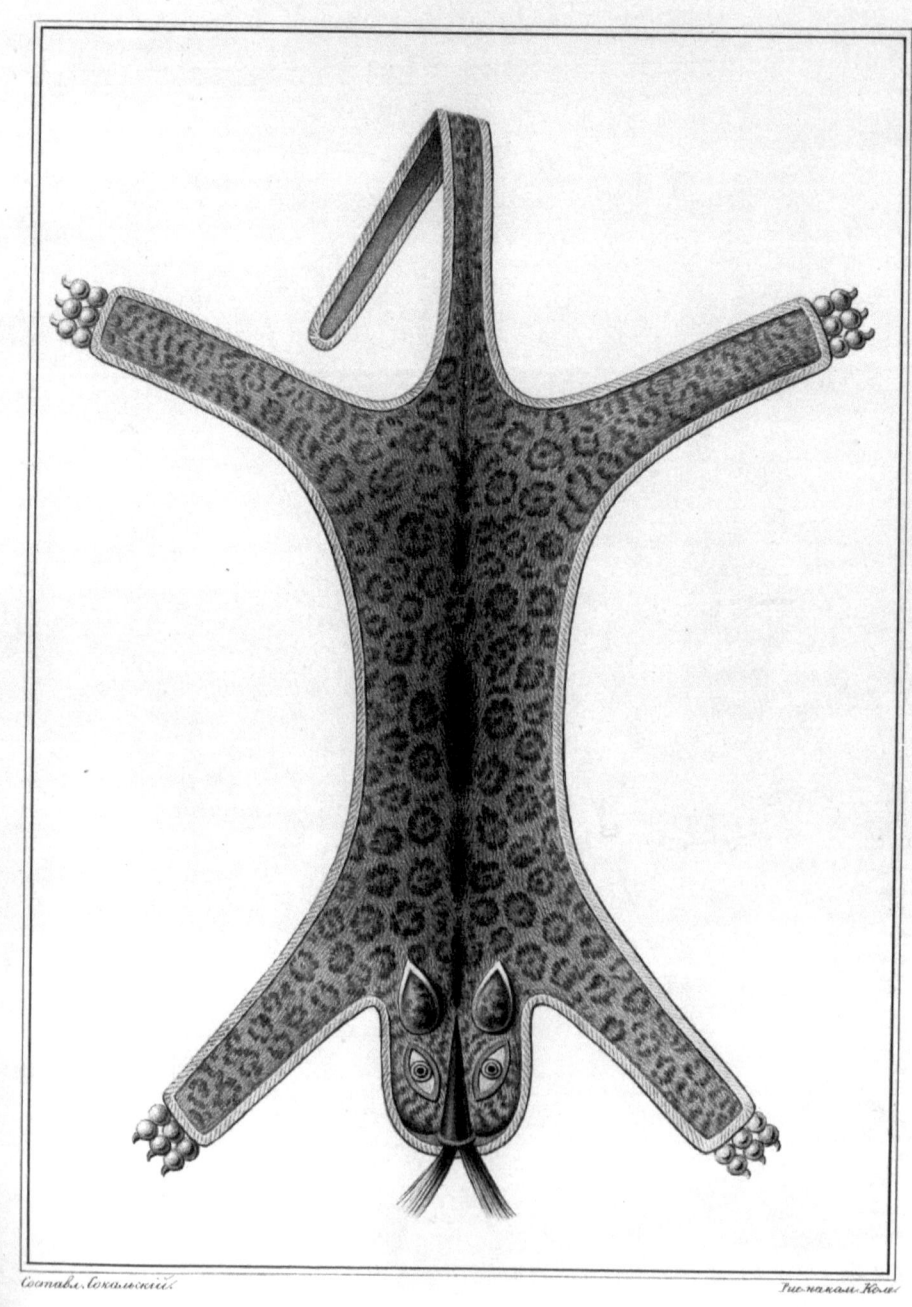

Leib-Hussar "Panther," 1796-1801.

Leib-Hussar Officers' sarsam horse decoration, 1796-1801.

1130.

Private and NCO. Leib-Hussar Regiment, 1796-1798. (In everyday uniform.)

Officer. Leib-Hussar Regiment, 1796-1798. (In everyday uniform.)

Officer. Leib-Hussar Regiment, 1796-1798. (In vengerka.)

Officer and Private. Leib-Hussar Regiment, 1799.

Officer and Private. Leib-Hussar Regiment, 1800-1801.

1185.

Privates. Leib-Cossack Regiment, 1796-1801.

Trumpeter, Non-Commissioned Officer, and Staff-Trumpeter. Leib-Cossack Regiment, 1796-1801.

Officer. Leib-Cossack Regiment, 1796-1801.

Officer and Private. Leib-Cossack Regiment, 1796-1801. (In winter uniform.)

Field-Grade Officer and Fireworker. Life-Guards Artillery Battalion, 1800-1801.

Cadets. 1st Cadet Corps, 1797-1799. (Musketeer and Grenadier.)

Company-Grade Officer. 1st Cadet Corps, 1797-1799.

1192.

Cadets. Boys' Section of the Army (later 1st) Cadet Corps. 1797-1801. (In summer uniform.)

Cadets. Boys' Section of the Army (later 1st) Cadet Corps. 1797-1801. (In winter uniform.)

1194.

Officer and Cadet. 2nd Cadet Corps, 1797-1800.

1195.

Cadet. IMPERIAL Military Orphans' Home, 1798-1801.

1196.

Pupil from soldiers' children. IMPERIAL Military Orphans' Home, 1798-1801.

Student. Military Orphans' Sections, 1798-1801.

Company-Grade Officer. IMPERIAL Military Orphans' Home, 1798-1801.

Cadet and Field-Grade Officer. 1st, 2nd, and Shklov Cadet Corps, 1800-1801.

1900.

Private of the 1st, and Officer of the 2nd. Chuguev Reg., 1798-1800. (In winter uniform.)

Privates. Teptyar Regiments, 1798-1801.

1802.

Cossack and Officer. Leib-Ural Sotnia, 1798-1801.

Ranker (sherengovyi). Lithuanian-Tatar Horse Regiment, 1797-1801.

Non-Commissioned Officer (namestnik) and Comrade (tovarishch). Lithuanian-Tatar Horse Regiment, 1797-1801. (In summer uniform.)

Officer. Lithuanian-Tatar Horse Regiment, 1797-1801. (In summer uniform.)

NCO and Officer. Lithuanian-Tatar Horse Regiment, 1797-1801. (In winter uniform.)

Ranker and Comrade. Lithuanian-Tatar Horse Regiment, 1797-1801. (In winter uniform.)

Comrade. Polish Horse Regiment, 1797-1801.

Officer and Non-Commissioned Officer. Polish Horse Regiment, 1797-1801.

Non-Commissioned Officer and Private. Balaklava Greek Infantry Battalion, 1797-1830.

Officer. Balaklava Greek Infantry Battalion, 1797-1801.

1212.

Musketeer and Officer. Prince de Condé's French Noble Regiment, 1797-1800.

1813.

Officer and NCO Duke de Bourbon's French Grenadier Regiment, 1797-1800.

Field-Grade Officer. Duke de Hohenlohe's German Regiment, 1797-1800.

Officer and Private. Duke de Berry's Noble Dragoon Regiment, 1797-1800.

1816.

Non-Commissioned Officer and Officer. Duke d'Enghien's Dragoon Regiment, 1797-1800.

Feldjäger and Feldjäger Officer. 1797-1801.

1218.

Officer in standard Army uniform for Infantry, 1796-1801.

1219.

Officer in standard Army uniform for Cavalry, 1796-1801.

Officer. Military Collegium and Commissariat and Provisions Departments, 1797-1801.

Official. Military Collegium and Commissariat and Provisions Departments, 1800-1801.

General-Adjutant and Aide-de-Camp. Infantry, 1796-1801.

Aide-de-Camp and General-Adjutant. Cavalry, 1796-1801.

WORK PLAN

Our reprint in based on the original 19th century volumes, to be precise the volumes from 7 to 9 are dedicated to the reign of Paul I; this first part is distributed on 7 volumes, having a numbering from 1 to 7. From number 10 to 18 of the original volumes, the second part is dedicated to the Russian troops under Alexander I. These still being worked on and they will be soon ready, distributed on twenty volumes approximately. Our new edition, the first ever published in English, both on paper and digital format, boasts a large number of color plates, many of them unpublished and coloured by our team of expert artists and scholars of uniformology. Each volume is based on 50/70 plates, always accompanied by the original translated text which describes the uniforms, the organization and the armament of the Russian army of the period.

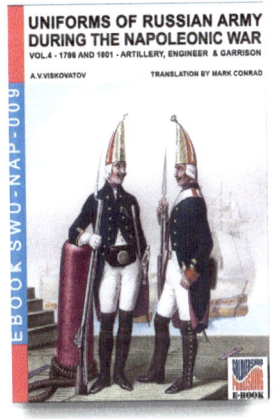

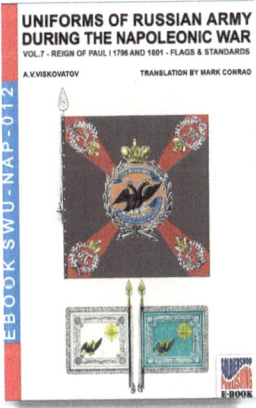